FOOTBALL
LEGENDS

CRISTIANO RONALDO

GEORGE MAUDSLEY

T0383290

FOOTBALL LEGENDS
CRISTIANO RONALDO

SCHOLASTIC

Published in the UK by Scholastic, 2024
1 London Bridge, London, SE1 9BG
Scholastic Ireland, 89E Lagan Road, Dublin Industrial Estate,
Glasnevin, Dublin, D11 HP5F

SCHOLASTIC and associated logos are trademarks
and/or registered trademarks of Scholastic Inc.

Text © George Maudsley, 2024
Cover illustration © Stanley Chow, 2024

The right of George Maudsley to be identified as the author
of this work has been asserted by him in accordance
with the Copyright, Designs and Patents Act, 1988.

ISBN 978 0702 33886 1

A CIP catalogue record for this book is available from the British Library.

All rights reserved.
This book is sold subject to the condition that it shall not,
by way of trade or otherwise, be lent, hired out or otherwise circulated in any
formof binding or cover other than that in which it is published. No part of
this publicationmay be reproduced, stored in a retrieval system, or transmitted
in any form or by anyother means (electronic, mechanical, photocopying,
recording or otherwise) without prior written permission of Scholastic Limited.

Printed and bound in Great Britain by Clays Ltd, Elcograf S.p.A

Paper made from wood grown in sustainable
forests and other controlled sources.

1 3 5 7 9 10 8 6 4 2

While this book is based on real characters and actual historical events,
some situations are fictional, created by the author.

UNAUTHORIZED: this book is not sponsored, approved
or endorsed by any person who appears in this book.

www.scholastic.co.uk

Contents

PARIS, 2016

The stadium was a cauldron of noise. Light from camera phones flashed all around like exploding fireworks. Most were aimed at one man, the Portuguese football team's captain. And he wasn't even on the pitch.

He stood near the touchline, waving his arms and clapping his hands in a whirr of motion as he urged his team on. They were 1-0 up in the dying minutes of extra time in the 2016 European Championship final. They simply had to hold on for the win – a victory that would be the greatest in Portugal's sporting history.

The opponents were the tournament's hosts, France, who attacked and attacked again, desperately searching for an equalizer. Time ticked down. Great players such as Antoine Griezmann and Paul Pogba tried their hardest, but Portugal stood strong.

Their captain was anxious. He had been forced off with an injury in the first half of the biggest match of his life, and he was worried he'd let his country down. So how could he help them best? By cheering them on and offering words of advice and encouragement. "Stick together! Fight to the end!" he shouted. Standing in the coach's technical area, it looked like he was the team's manager!

The assistant referee told him to sit back down. He hopped back to his seat but struggled to contain his nerves. Portugal were so close now! France had the ball back again as Anthony Martial tried to run past Cédric. The defender refused to let him.

It was too much: Portugal's captain was too far away from the action. He had to do something to get his team over the line. He hobbled forward and barked instructions to his teammates as time ticked away. There were seconds to go. The rest of the substitutes and the coaching staff joined him on the touchline.

As the final whistle eventually blew and Portugal became champions of Europe for the first time, their captain fell to the ground, engulfed in a huge hug from one of the coaching staff. Against all odds, they had done it! This was the greatest moment of the player's career, the biggest moment in his country's footballing history. Tears ran down the side of his face as he cried in disbelief and pride.

He had achieved so much in his life, and he hoped there would be much more to come, but this was undoubtedly the pinnacle, something he had dreamed of since he was a small child living so very far from the bright lights of any big football stadium.

He was the greatest football player in the world, and he had just helped accomplish his nation's greatest achievement. His name was Cristiano Ronaldo.

A STAR IS BORN

On 5 February 1985, on a small Portuguese island in the Atlantic Ocean, many miles from the northwest coast of Africa, Cristiano Ronaldo dos Santos Aveiro was born. As he lay sleeping in his mother Dolores' arms in the hospital in Funchal, Madeira's capital, the baby's father, Dinis, looked down fondly at his new son.

"I've been thinking about what to call him. I'd like to name him after the American president," he said.

"Ronald Reagan?" Dolores asked.

"Yes, you know he was my favourite actor.

He's amazing!"

"OK. Ronaldo, then. *Cristiano* Ronaldo," she said.

Dinis smiled. "Cristiano Ronaldo. I like it. It sounds like a sportsman's name."

Cristiano was the youngest of four children. His sister Elma and brother, Hugo, were twelve and ten years older respectively, and his other sister, Katia, was eight. Unfortunately, the Aveiro family did not have much money. Dolores' job as a cook and Dinis' as a gardener only just made enough to put food on the table. There were no presents or toys at Christmas. The children slept on the hard floor of one room in their unpainted brick-and-wood house, the roof of which leaked during storms, and their parents slept in the other. Clothes were donated from cousins and other families.

But these things never got little Cristiano down. His parents always made sure he felt safe and loved. The boy was usually found outside, playing in the steep, uneven streets and kicking a ball with the other kids.

"Cristiano! Come back in and do your

homework!" Katia cried. But her younger brother had dumped his rucksack and was off and away the moment he got in from school. She watched him performing tricks with another kid's ball, juggling it and zipping round the boys as he dribbled from one end of their sloped pitch to the other. "Not bad ..." she muttered to herself.

One day, his godfather, Fernão Sousa, the captain of a small local team called Andorinha, bought Cristiano his own football. The boy couldn't believe it. "For me?" he asked.

Fernão winked. "I remembered how badly you wanted one last year."

Cristiano would play until dark, and if there was no one else around, would kick the ball for hours against a wall by a small field nearby. As he did, his mind drifted away to far-off stadiums and roaring crowds. *I can beat all the kids in the street*, he thought. *Maybe one day I could do it on a real pitch*.

When he took his ball to school one day, his teacher was not impressed. "That ball isn't going to put food on the table, Cristiano. It won't get you anywhere in life. Studying hard in school is the only way you'll ever achieve anything."

I'll show you, he said to himself.

THE LITTLE BEE

Dinis dumped the cones and football bag by the front door. He watched his eight-year-old son laugh as he performed yet another trick in a game against the other kids, the ball seemingly stuck to his foot. "We're going to have to do something about that," he said to Dolores as she popped her head outside. "Cristiano! Come over here for a minute!"

"But, Dad, I'm on a double hat-trick!" Cristiano complained as he trudged over.

Dinis couldn't help but laugh. As well as being a gardener, Dinis worked at Andorinha football club as a part-time kit man. "How would you like to come down to the club with me next week and take part in a training session?"

Cristiano couldn't have been more excited. The following week, Dinis and Cristiano turned up at Andorinha, with the boy raring to go. He stared at the cones, the kids stretching and the proper football kits. It felt like the real thing.

That day, Cristiano performed well enough to be invited back again. His street skills were paying off. He was soon a regular, playing with children two or three years older. To little Cristiano, the other kids looked twice his size, but that didn't stop him – it just made him want to beat them even more!

He was never afraid to get on the ball, dribble and perform his lightning-fast stepovers. He soon earned everyone's respect and became a very important player for Andorinha. He even won a trophy for player of the tournament in a local competition! "He's so fast! Like a little bee!" one of his teammates shouted during training. The nickname stuck.

During one game, Andorinha were winning 3-0. The Little Bee was playing brilliantly, weaving in and out of defenders with his tricks and fast feet. Unfortunately, he clashed heads with another player and had to go off. Andorinha lost 4-3.

Cristiano hated having to miss any football, but he hated losing even more. In one game, he went into the dressing room at half-time in tears because his team were 2-0 down.

"Why are you crying, Cristiano?" his coach asked him.

"Because we are losing!" the boy replied.

"Well, show them how much you care on the pitch instead!"

And show them he did. He single-handedly turned the game around to win 3-2.

His performances were getting noticed. Word soon reached Nacional, one of the biggest clubs on the island, who had been in Portugal's top league only a few years before. They sent their youth-team coach down to watch Cristiano. It was none other than his godfather, Fernão. He knew his godson played football, but couldn't believe how good he was! Before long, he'd signed the now ten-year-old Little Bee up – Fernão just couldn't let him get away. He knew Nacional was the best place for his godson to get even better.

Cristiano was amazed. This was the first time he'd come into contact with a real academy. The coaches pushed him in training, which the young boy threw himself into with huge enthusiasm. When he wasn't training, he was still playing on the street – he'd often spend ten or twelve hours a day with a ball!

CD NACIONAL

Club name: Clube Desportivo Nacional
Nickname: Alvinegros (White and Blacks), Nacionalistas (Nationalists)
Founded: 1910
Current league: Liga Portugal 1
Ground: Estádio da Madeira (5,132 capacity)
Colours: Black-and-white stripes

At this point, Cristiano wanted to do everything on the pitch himself. It was at Nacional that he received his first real lessons in tactics. "Look, you're playing in this position, so this is what your movement should be like," one of his coaches told him in one training session. "You score lots of goals already but think how many more you could score if you let your teammates help you more."

Cristiano loved scoring goals. The more he scored, the more he wanted. And he still loved to perform his skills. In one match, he ran the length of the field, controlling the ball without it touching the ground once!

Even illness couldn't slow Cristiano down ahead of an Under-13 championship decider. "Mum, I want to play," he begged Dolores. "If I feel ill, I'll ask to be taken off."

Dolores could see there was no stopping him. That day, he scored a goal and Nacional became the champions – his first team trophy. "Yeeesss!" he cried, as he held the trophy high. I could get used to this feeling, he thought.

But after just two seasons, he was ready to leave Nacional. Sporting CP had come calling.

THE TRIAL

Fernão, Cristiano's godfather, could see the boy had quickly outgrown Nacional and Madeira. He knew Cristiano needed a bigger club that could help fulfil his potential, and that meant going to mainland Portugal. Using his contacts, a trial at the mighty Sporting, one of Portugal's biggest clubs, was arranged.

It was a big step for the twelve-year-old. He had never left Madeira or been on a plane. And he would be flying alone.

The night before, Cristiano couldn't sleep a wink. He lay in bed, thinking about the trial. *If I show them what I can do, I know they will like me*, he thought in the darkness.

Arriving in Lisbon with a name tag around his neck, he was met by Aurélio Pereira, the man in charge of transfers at Sporting. Aurélio drove him through the busy streets of Portugal's capital to where he would be staying. "It's like being in a different country," he said on the phone to Dolores that evening.

"Just do your best and enjoy it, Cristiano. Be yourself." Dolores tried to hide the fact she was already missing her little boy.

Cristiano was very nervous but didn't let go of his self-belief. On the day of the trial, he warmed up in his Sporting kit with the boys from the academy. As the session got underway, the ball came over to him. He prepared to control it … but it went under his foot! *Keep calm,* he thought. *I'm going to do this.*

On the sideline stood Paulo Cardoso and Osvaldo Silva, two of the coaches, who would be writing a report on Cristiano. When the Madeiran next received the ball, he took off at an electric pace and started dribbling past the other kids, many a couple of years older. The two men looked at each other. "What is this?" they both said. They were witnessing something special.

The next day, Aurélio went to see Cristiano play

himself. He was stunned at this skinny twelve-year-old who showed no fear of the older boys. "We have to sign him up!" he told the other coaches.

Back in Madeira, Dolores and Dinis had a choice to make. Could they let their young son leave to live all on his own in a far-away city? "Let me go, Mum," begged Cristiano.

His parents looked at each other. They knew they couldn't get in the way of this, as much as they'd miss him. "Go, fight for your dream, son," Dolores said through her tears.

Lisbon awaited.

SPORTING CP

Club name: Sporting Clube de Portugal
Nickname: Leões (Lions)
Founded: 1906
Current league: Primeira Liga
Ground: Ground: Estádio José Alvalade (50,095 capacity)
Colours: Green and white

LISBON

Cristiano was now a player in the Sporting academy. In a strange city where he didn't know anybody, life was tough for him. Most of the boys were a couple of years older. In fact, Cristiano was the only twelve-year-old in the team. His Madeiran accent marked him out and was the source of some cruel jokes from the other kids at school and at the academy. He missed his mum, and in the evenings, with no football to play, he would feel homesick. When he called home, he was often in tears.

"Don't listen to them, Cristiano. Do your talking on the pitch," Dolores would tell him.

So he worked as hard as he could in training, showed his abilities, and before long had earned everyone's respect: the jokes stopped. He was even moved up a year-group to challenge himself further.

As time went by, Cristiano made a circle of close friends who would spend their time eating out, training and exploring the city. Sometimes this got them into trouble. One night, four of them were approached by a gang. Two of Cristiano's friends ran off, but Cristiano stayed and stood up to the muggers. He was determined to show leadership and strength, even in the scariest moments.

Cristiano was impressing the coaches with his efforts in training. He worked harder than anyone else, and stayed behind to practise his free kicks, corners and dribbles. When he was back in Funchal on his holidays, he even ran with weights strapped to his ankles to build up strength! He loved spending time in the gym, and would sneak out at night, hop over a fence, climb through a window and use the equipment when the place was closed. "Come on, José, now is our chance. If we don't put the effort in, how can we be the best?" whispered Cristiano, nudging his friend José

Semedo to wake him up.

They were frequently caught using the weights and running on the treadmills, with the Under-16/17 coach Luís Martins called down to collect them. "If you work too hard, you might injure yourself!" he warned.

Cristiano's desire and determination could not be stopped. But one day, even he had to take things a bit easier. During training, he felt something strange in his chest. "It's my heart," he told the coaches. "Sometimes I can feel it racing and it makes me suddenly tired." The doctors were as concerned as the coaches, and it was decided he would have surgery.

In June 2000, the surgeons used a laser to correct parts of the fifteen-year-old's heart. Thankfully, he returned home the next day and, with a bit of time off, was back training as hard as ever. Not even surgery could hold him back.

BREAKTHROUGH

"Cristiano, get yourself ready. You'll be training with the first team this afternoon."

Cristiano was sixteen years old and couldn't believe his ears. He called his mum straight away. "Can you believe it, Mum? It might finally be happening!" Dolores couldn't have been prouder of her son.

Cristiano was full of nerves as the training session approached. He watched the older players getting ready, barely taking any notice of him. *I have to show them what I can do*, he told himself. But that day, Cristiano found out what it took to be a first-team player. While he didn't do badly, he didn't excel either, which was a new experience for the Madeiran. It was the same the next time he trained with them. They were all useful lessons, though, and Cristiano redoubled his efforts in the gym and in training with the Under-17s.

After a few months he felt like he had got up to speed. *Time to express myself*, he thought. He nutmegged a senior player, dribbled past another with a burst of speed and buried a shot into the bottom corner. "That's the way, Cristiano!" shouted first-team coach László Bölöni.

He didn't stop there. He went steaming into a tackle on an older player. "Calm it, kid," the man said.

"We'll see if you still call me that when I'm the best player in the world!" he replied.

László raised an eyebrow and muttered to one of the other coaches, "The lad doesn't lack for ambition, does he?"

Cristiano was doing double muscle-building sessions and staying late practising his shooting – he was determined to keep getting better and prove his worth to László. It worked: his progress was astonishing, and he played for the Under-16s, the Under-17s, the Under-18s, the reserves and first team in the same season! But it wouldn't be until the next season, 2002/03, that he became a regular first-team player.

He made his debut as a substitute against Inter Milan in a Champions League qualifying game on 14 August 2002. It ended 0-0, but the excitement Cristiano felt was immense. He couldn't believe he was now playing in packed stadiums against massive clubs!

His league debut swiftly followed against Braga. Next up was a game against Moreirense. With the score at 1-0 to Sporting, Cristiano received the ball fifty yards from goal and took off. He accelerated past the desperate lunging tackles of two Moreirense players and approached the penalty area at top speed; he made a quick stepover and touch to take the ball away from a defender, a dinked shot past the onrushing goalkeeper, and ... GOOOAAAALLL! His first goal as a professional footballer!

Cristiano was beside himself with joy. His

teammates mobbed him, ruffling his hair and shouting, "Amazing, Cristiano! Wow, what a goal!"

In the stands, his mother fainted. On the touchline, László beamed and shook the hand of one of his coaching staff. Cristiano had arrived.

He scored another goal in that game and went on to make thirty-one appearances, scoring five goals in total, that season.

Already, other clubs were starting to hear of this wonderkid from Madeira. Offers were coming in from the likes of Liverpool, Valencia and Parma. "Wow, do they like me that much?" he asked his new agent, Jorge Mendes, in disbelief.

"Cristiano, everyone likes you. But we have to be careful about your next step. It has to be the right move for your progression."

Cristiano even travelled to London to see Arsenal's training ground and to meet the club's legendary manager, Arsène Wenger. In the end, they couldn't offer enough money.

And then Manchester United came to town.

THE GAME THAT CHANGED EVERYTHING

Sporting were due to play Manchester United in a friendly on 6 August 2003 to unveil their new stadium. Cristiano was buzzing with excitement.

"I'm going to be playing against legends like Paul Scholes and Ruud van Nistelrooy!" he said to his mum before the game. "This is my chance to test myself against the best!"

That night, eighteen-year-old Cristiano gave United's stars the run-around, especially right-back John O'Shea, who was twisted inside out as Cristiano dribbled this way and that, bursting past with blistering speed to unleash ferocious shots or clever passes. The crowd cheered every time Cristiano touched the ball. He was having the game of his life.

His performance had made the United players in the dugout sit up and take notice. "Who is this guy?" Ryan Giggs asked. A few joked that Cristiano's tricks were making John dizzy because he was so confused by the speed of Cristiano's feet.

Sporting won the match 3-1. "We've got to sign him up, boss!" Rio Ferdinand and Scholes said to the manager, Sir Alex Ferguson. The Scotsman looked at them and smiled. He had a plan.

In fact, a deal had been agreed the night before, and the match had been Cristiano's chance to show just what United would be getting. He had not disappointed. Sir Alex later said, "Ronaldo was a revelation. It was the biggest surge of excitement and anticipation I experienced in football management." High praise indeed.

Cristiano's dreams were coming true. He would be off to Manchester, home of the English champions.

MANCHESTER UNITED

Club name: Manchester United
Nickname: The Red Devils, United
Founded: 1878
Current league: Premier League
Ground: Old Trafford (74,310 capacity)
Colours: Red, white and black

THE NEW
NUMBER SEVEN

The deal for Cristiano had included a plan to loan him back to the Lisbon side for a year before moving permanently to Manchester. Once Sir Alex had seen him play, however, that idea was scrapped – he wanted him immediately!

Just a few days later, Cristiano was on a plane to England. Despite Sir Alex's plans, Cristiano still believed he would be loaned back to Sporting. He turned up to sign his contract without a suitcase!

Cristiano also visited the Carrington training ground, where he bumped into John O'Shea, the defender he had tormented in the match for

Sporting. "You owe me part of your transfer fee for getting you the move here!" John joked. Cristiano laughed. *I think I'm going to like it here*, he said to himself.

One big surprise still lay in store. As they sat in the car, Sir Alex asked him what shirt number he'd like to wear.

"Number twenty-eight is fine. No one is using it, and it's the one I wore at Sporting."

"Well, I've got news for you, son. You're going to be wearing seven."

Cristiano was dumbstruck. That was the shirt worn by George Best, Eric Cantona and David Beckham – some of United's biggest legends! He would have to work harder than ever to show everyone he deserved it.

THE UNITED NUMBER SEVEN SHIRT

Manchester United's number-seven shirt has been made famous by some of the club's greatest ever players. George Best, an incredible dribbler of the ball who was for decades thought of as United's best ever, first made the number famous. In the 1990s, Eric Cantona, the genius Frenchman, helped United win the league for the first time in twenty-six years, and went on to win many more trophies wearing the shirt. When he left, David Beckham was given the number, and carried on Cantona's legacy by winning many more league titles as well as the Treble – their national league competition, the main country cup and Europe's main club trophy – in 1999. It would be a big shirt for an eighteen-year-old Cristiano to fill.

Just ten days after the game in Lisbon, Cristiano was getting ready to make his Manchester United debut. As he stood on the touchline and saw his new number flash up on the assistant referee's electronic board, he heard the noise and excitement go up a level. A shudder of anticipation went through him. United were playing Bolton at Old Trafford, and at 1-0 to the home side, the match was still in the balance.

When Cristiano came on, he gave the fans exactly what they wanted to see: pace, trickery and a desire to attack. He was a classic United forward. "Brilliant, Cristiano!" the captain, Roy Keane, yelled after the younger man turned and powered away from two Bolton midfielders. One moment he'd release Ryan Giggs down the left, the next he'd be putting in a cross for Ruud van Nistelrooy. He was everywhere. At one point, Roy fed Cristiano in on the left of the box; the Portuguese cut inside and … foul! Kevin Nolan dragged him down, bamboozled by Cristiano's skills.

"Yes! It's a penalty!" Cristiano cried.

He helped his new team to a 4-0 win and picked up the Man of the Match award in the process. He'd loved every minute, especially hearing the fans' excitement every time he touched the ball.

"That was brilliant!" Sir Alex said after the game. There were slaps on the back from all his new teammates, and the papers were full of discussion about United's new number seven. Cristiano was on cloud nine.

ADAPTING

Cristiano spent much of his first season at United learning that the English game was very different to that in Portugal. Even in training, Roy or Paul Scholes would put in big tackles on him. He got used to being sent to the ground. "Perhaps this is because I do too many tricks on them?" he asked Sir Alex one day.

"Just keep doing what you're doing, son. We'll look after you," his manager told him. Cristiano knew he'd have to continue to work hard – just because he'd got the move to a big club didn't mean he should put in less effort. How else would he achieve his goal of being the best?

He made sure he was the first to arrive at the Carrington training ground each morning and would leave late. He'd set up his own exercises, and practise free kicks and shots over and over again. He also realized that he needed to be stronger and more powerful if he was to stop defenders pushing him off the ball. One day he found the power development coach, Mike Clegg, in the gym. "I'm going to be the best in the world and you're going to help me," Cristiano told him. Cristiano saw that Mike was someone else who was as committed to achieving perfection as he was. Together, they would spend the next few years improving Cristiano's fitness and strength, maximizing his power on the pitch.

On 1 November 2003, Cristiano had a game against Portsmouth. As he stood over the ball on the left-hand side of the pitch to take a free kick, he planted his legs wide apart in what would become a familiar stance. He ran up and curled a low, powerful cross into the box. Defenders, attackers and even the keeper stretched to reach … it missed them all and went in! His first

United goal! As he ran away in delight, Roy and Gary Neville chased him to share the moment. "Brilliant, Cristiano! Well done!" they shouted in his ear. What a feeling! He needed to experience this again.

He would be in and out of the team that season as he continued his development under Sir Alex's watchful eye. But he was picked to start in the FA Cup final against Millwall and had an opportunity to help the team win their only chance of silverware. *This is my biggest match so far. I have to bring my top game.*

And he did just that. Cristiano was exceptional that day. He used all the lessons he'd learned so far – when to make runs, when to pass, when to shoot. And then, just before half-time, his moment came. Gary put a high cross in, and who was there to meet it? Cristiano! A late run and header down into the ground netted him an FA Cup final goal! "Yesssss!" he yelled as he ran off to celebrate.

The team triumphed 3-0 and Cristiano won his first ever senior team trophy. He hoped it would be the first of many.

He also discovered he would be in Portugal's squad for Euro 2004. It was yet another chance for him to impress.

A NEAR MISS

Portugal were the hosts of the 2004 European Championship, and were drawn in a group with Greece, Russia and Spain. The first game did not go well for Portugal, who surprisingly lost 2-1 to the defensive Greeks, although Cristiano scored an injury-time goal as a substitute. It should have been a big moment for Cristiano, but he couldn't feel happy when his country had lost.

After a 2-0 victory over Russia, Cristiano's play off the bench had earned him his first ever start for his country for the final group game against neighbours Spain. It was a must-win. And win they did, with a brilliant performance from the eighteen-year-old. "Ronaldo is the future," wrote the papers. Next up was England in the quarter-finals.

A tense match ended 2-2 after extra time, meaning it was time for penalties. Deco and Simão had already scored when Cristiano stepped up. *Ignore the noise of the fans, Cristiano. Focus,* he told himself. To the crowd he looked confident. Inside, he was tense. A halting run up, and BANG! Up near the top left-hand corner – goal! All those practice penalties had paid off.

After England's Darius Vassell missed and Portugal's goalkeeper Ricardo scored, the hosts were through. Time for the Netherlands in the semis.

Cristiano played brilliantly again, scoring another header from a Luís Figo corner. Portugal won 2-1. "We're in the final! Come on!" chanted Cristiano alongside his teammates. What a buzz for an eighteen-year-old!

The final was poised to be a rematch with Greece, against whom Portugal had lost in the group games. The game was nervy and tight. Once again, Greece found a way through, with a goal from Angelos Charisteas in the fifty-seventh minute. The match ended 1-0, with Greece the victors despite only achieving one shot on target. It was a devastating loss for Portugal and Cristiano. As his coach, Luiz Felipe Scolari, hugged him after the match, he whispered, "We may have lost, but you have been a winner in this tournament. Keep it up – I know there will be much more to come from you."

Cristiano appreciated his words. He would use the experience to keep improving. For now, it was home to Manchester.

A CHEEKY WINK

Cristiano's next two seasons for Manchester United were another learning curve. United finished third in the league and lost the FA Cup final to Arsenal in 2004/05, but won the League Cup in 2005/06, with Cristiano scoring the fourth goal in United's 4-0 victory over Wigan Athletic in the final. Chelsea won the league in both seasons. Cristiano still wasn't a guaranteed starter, making a similar number of appearances as in his first season at the club, and scoring only a few more goals. But he knew there was plenty to come if he kept working hard.

A HELPING HAND

Cristiano is known for his charity work and care for other people. When he heard about the tsunami that devastated Indonesia in 2004, he wanted to visit the area to see how he could help.

While he was there, he met a young boy called Martunis who had been found wearing a Portugal football shirt after being stranded alone on a beach for twenty-one days. Cristiano was amazed by the boy's strength and the pair struck up a friendship, with Cristiano promising to pay for his education. The footballer also helped Martunis get signed to Real Madrid Foundation's football school in his local town. Eleven years after the tsunami, Cristiano's aid was to pay off when Martunis was signed by Sporting Lisbon's academy, making the dreams of someone who had lost nearly everything come true.

The summer of 2006 was Cristiano's first World Cup, which was to be held in Germany. Portugal won all of their group games, including a goal for Cristiano against Iran, slingshotting them through to the second round. After a 1-0 win against the Netherlands, they again found themselves in a quarter-final with England.

The game was closely fought, with both sides struggling to take charge. The key moment came in the sixty-second minute. England's Wayne Rooney, Cristiano's United club mate, appeared to stamp on Portuguese defender Ricardo Carvalho.

Cristiano couldn't believe it. He ran up to the referee to check the official would protect his teammate in such a big moment. "Ref, what was that?! That has to be a red card!" cried Cristiano.

Wayne wasn't happy with his club mate's questions. He gave Cristiano a soft push, but the referee's mind was made up. He'd already seen everything. He reached into his pocket and held his hand to the sky. In it was a red card.

As Wayne received his marching orders, Cristiano got some new instructions from the coaches. He winked to say he understood. The television cameras – beamed into English fans' living rooms – only showed the wink. The supporters were furious. *He's got our player sent off by complaining to the referee!* they thought. They were not going to let this go.

Back on the pitch, Cristiano tried to remain focused. Portugal pushed and pushed, but the English defence kept them out. The match finished 0-0 after extra time, so penalties would decide the winner. The English had never won a World Cup shoot-out and wanted to get their own back after losing to Portugal this way two years earlier.

The Madeiran had been given the fifth spot kick and, with Portugal 2-1 up in the shoot-out after four each, knew he could send Portugal into the semis. *Remember what you practised. It was all for this,* he thought to himself as he walked up to the spot. He kissed the ball and put it down. He puffed out his cheeks. Here we go. BANG! He sent the keeper the wrong way – he'd done it! He screamed to the sky in celebration as his teammates went wild.

After the match, it was clear there was uproar in the media about the wink. Cristiano spoke to Wayne and another United player, Rio Ferdinand, in the dressing rooms. "I didn't wink like they're saying," he said.

"Look, let's just act as normal as we can, but people are going to be angry," said Wayne. He was right.

Even though Portugal lost 1-0 to France in the semi-final, it did not stop a wave of criticism coming for Cristiano. He even wondered whether he would be able to stay at Manchester United next season. But Wayne kept in touch with him all summer and, as ever, Sir Alex was by his side – with their support, he knew he'd be able to carry on. However come the new season, England fans would not be so forgiving.

FINDING ANOTHER LEVEL

Cristiano was booed during the first few away matches of the 2006/07 season. But something had changed. This was a new Cristiano, for whom the thousands of hours of training and gym work was now paying off – as was Sir Alex's faith in him. Everyone could see he was stronger, faster and more powerful than before. Was he finally going to fulfil his potential?

"Mike, I feel ready. Other players are bouncing off *me* now!" he told Mike Clegg.

Cristiano's performances in those first few games silenced the critics, creating a buzz of excitement among his teammates.

"It's going to be a good season," Wayne predicted after training one day.

Starting with a 5-1 thrashing of Fulham on the opening day of the season through to a 7-1 humbling of Roma in the Champions League in April, United found themselves in with a chance of the Treble. They were right at the top of the Premier League, and had a European semi-final against AC Milan and the FA Cup final against Chelsea to look forward to.

Cristiano was having his best goal-scoring season ever. In the return fixture away at Fulham, he even ran from his own half to score! His relationships on the pitch with Wayne, Ryan and Louis Saha were causing havoc for every opponent. Cristiano's reliance on tricks and stepovers, and his mistimed passes were replaced with deadly focus. He felt unstoppable.

The first leg of a classic Champions League semi-final at Old Trafford, against an AC Milan side that included stars such as Kaká, Paolo Maldini, Andrea Pirlo and Clarence Seedorf, finished 4-3 to United. It included a Cristiano goal and a Wayne double. "Brilliant, lads! We're in the driving seat," Sir Alex said in the dressing room afterwards.

Unfortunately, Milan showed their quality in the second leg with a 3-0 win to knock United out, but, with a couple more victories in the league, they got the points they needed for the title. Cristiano was a champion for the first time! He couldn't believe it. "We are the champions!" he sang with his teammates.

"Congratulations, son. You played a big part in this. I expect even more next season!" said Sir Alex the next day. The manager knew they could never take their eyes off the ball, even in victory.

The last game of the season was the FA Cup final. Sadly, Chelsea nicked it with a 1-0 win. While it was disappointing to lose in the semi-final in Europe and now the final in the Cup, it had been a brilliant season, especially for Cristiano. He netted twenty-three goals in all competitions and was named Player of the Year and Young Player of the Year by the Professional Footballers' Association.

Despite all this, Cristiano's journey to the top was only just beginning.

CONQUERING EUROPE

Cristiano's progression during the 2007/08 season was staggering. With some private lessons from René Meulensteen, one of Sir Alex's assistants, he became even more ruthless in front of goal. Was he finally about to achieve his dream of becoming the best player in the world? By the end of January of that season, he had already scored a staggering twenty-seven goals, including his first hat-trick against Newcastle United.

"You're way more than a winger now, Cristiano!" said injured captain Gary Neville. "With you playing like this, we could win the Champions

League this time."

Roma were the opponents once again in the quarter-finals of the competition. In the away leg, United were playing the better football. It was time for Cristiano to show exactly how far he'd come. When Paul Scholes hung a cross from the right side of the box, it looked like no United player would reach it … until Cristiano came flying from nowhere to meet the ball with a bullet header. Fans and players alike were stunned. "That's one of the best headers I've ever seen," Wayne Rooney yelled as Cristiano lay on the ground. The Portuguese player had seemed to hang in mid-air as he jumped as high as the crossbar to connect with the ball. Another win at Old Trafford sent United to the semi-finals, where they would face Barcelona.

A tense game in Spain ended 0-0, meaning United had the home advantage for the second leg. "Come on, lads! We can do this!" shouted Rio Ferdinand in the tunnel before the teams headed out. The match was another close one, which was settled by a Paul Scholes wonder strike after fourteen minutes. They were heading to the final in Moscow.

Back in England, the league title would be

decided by the final game, which was against Wigan Athletic. If United won, they would be champions again; if they lost, Chelsea might pip them. Wigan started the game aggressively, having a couple of early shots. United slowly began to show their skills, however. A pass into the area was collected by Wayne, who was chopped down. Penalty! Up stepped Cristiano. *I know exactly where this is going*, he told himself. A fast run-up … and he slotted it past the keeper! 1-0!

"We're halfway there," said Paul at half-time. "Stick to what we're doing."

There was no need to worry. With ten minutes to go, Ryan Giggs drifted into the area and between two defenders to run neatly on to a pass from Wayne, before slotting the ball into the goal. 2-0! They were champions again! Now it was time for Moscow.

Their opponents, just as in the race for the league title, were Chelsea. United had the better of the first half, as Cristiano used his skills against Chelsea's Michael Essien, who was usually a midfielder but today was playing right-back. "Paul, Carrick, get the ball to me! I can beat this guy!" he said. In the twenty-sixth minute, Wes Brown sent in a cross from the right. And Cristiano was there to meet it, rising above Michael at the back post. "Come onnnnn!" he screamed. *Could we do this?*

Chelsea equalized in the last minute of the first half and were growing in strength in the second half, but couldn't get past United's well-organized defence. The match went to extra time as the tension increased, but still no more goals came. That meant penalties.

Both sides scored their first two. Next was Cristiano. *This is it*, he thought. *It has all led here. Let's do this!* He chose his spot, tried a stuttering run-up to unnerve Chelsea keeper Petr Čech, and struck the ball well … but it went straight at Petr! He'd missed. Cristiano couldn't believe it. He buried his face in his hands. He walked sadly back to his teammates, who put their arms around him. "Don't worry – it's not finished yet," they said.

Chelsea captain John Terry had the chance to win it for his side. He ran up but he slipped and his shot hit the post! United were back in with a chance. It was now sudden death – whoever missed would lose. United scored their next two. Then Chelsea striker Nicolas Anelka took his turn. Goalkeeper

Edwin van der Sar made himself as big as possible, puffing up his chest and spreading his arms wide. The ball was struck. Everything seemed to move in slow motion. Edwin dived to his right, reached for the ball – and saved it! Manchester United were champions of Europe!

As the United players all ran off to congratulate Edwin, Cristiano fell to the ground in relief and joy. *Thank goodness! I can't believe it,* he thought.

If the previous season had been a great one, then this one was out of this world. He had scored an incredible forty-two goals in all competitions, with thirty-one in the league alone. What's more, a few months later he was awarded the Ballon d'Or, the trophy for the world's best player. He had finally done it.

THE LONG GOODBYE

Although he had had the perfect season, Cristiano had always had one more ambition: to play in Spain for Real Madrid. Dolores had long admired the club, and her son was no different.

After the 2008 Champions League win, Cristiano made it known that he would like to make the move to Spain. He had achieved everything possible in Manchester. And, unsurprisingly, Madrid were very keen.

Speculation continued throughout the summer, including at Euro 2008 where Portugal, captained by Cristiano, went out at the quarter-final stage to

Germany. Eventually, Sir Alex convinced Cristiano to stay. "Just give us one more year, and if you play well and still want to go to Madrid, we'll let you."

"Everyone's been good to me in Manchester. I've loved it here and achieved all my dreams. Let's give it one more year," Cristiano agreed.

That season, 2008/09, was another good one for United, who won the Premier League for the third season in a row, as well as the League Cup. In Europe, they reached the final once again, where they faced an invigorated Barcelona side led by the inspirational Carles Puyol and managed by Pep Guardiola. Barcelona were brilliant that day, and defeated United 2-0.

THE PUSKÁS AWARD

The Puskás Award is given by FIFA to the scorer of the most impressive goal in each calendar year. It is named after Ferenc Puskás, the captain of the legendary Hungarian team of the 1950s. It was first awarded in 2009 and went to Cristiano in what was his final year at Manchester United.

The goal was one of his best ever. Picking up the ball more than forty yards from goal in a Champions League quarter-final at Porto, he unleashed a powerful shot from an incredible distance. His teammate Rio Ferdinand shouted at him not to shoot, but then found himself celebrating as it sailed into the net. The goal was the winner and sent United into the semis at the same time.

United kept their promise to Cristiano, who announced that, after six seasons, he would be heading to Spain to join Real Madrid.

It was sad saying goodbye to his United teammates. "You don't know how good you've got it here," Gary joked. "Good luck," said Rio, and he meant it. One chapter was closing, and an exciting one beginning.

REAL MADRID

Club name: Real Madrid
Nickname: Los Blancos (the Whites), Los Merengues (the Meringues)
Founded: 1902
Current league: La Liga
Ground: Estadio Santiago Bernabéu (85,000 capacity)
Colours: White

HALA MADRID

Cristiano was nervous for the first time in years. He was about to be unveiled to Real Madrid fans as their new number nine, and the world's most expensive signing, with a transfer fee of eighty million pounds. Anticipation had reached fever pitch.

As he waited in the tunnel to be called, he could barely hear himself think, the crowd was that loud.

Club president Florentino Pérez finally called his name and Cristiano skipped up the stairs and on to the pitch. He was dumbstruck. Eighty thousand people had turned up to see him – a record. Chants of "Ronaldo" filled the stadium. He had prepared a few words to say, but when he came towards the microphone, he couldn't remember them! He said whatever popped into his head: "My childhood dream of playing for Real Madrid has come true. I didn't expect this. It's amazing. Thank you very much. Now I ask you all to say with me ... I'm going to count to three and we'll all say, 'Hala Madrid!' OK? One, two, three ... Hala Madrid!" The crowd bellowed his words in unison.

If his unveiling as a new Madrid player had shown him anything, it was that these fans expected more than any others – it was the stuff of dreams, but also a huge challenge for Cristiano. Could he continue his great form here? Would he continue to progress?

The main challenge would be to knock Treble-winning Barcelona off their perch. To do so, Florentino had also brought in Kaká, Karim Benzema and Xabi Alonso.

Cristiano started his Madrid career promisingly with five goals in his first four games. Unfortunately, an injury at the end of September and a couple of suspensions did not allow him to show his true potential, but he still managed thirty-three goals in thirty-five appearances – his best numbers after his Ballon d'Or season two years before. The team had a good league campaign, finishing on their best-ever points tally of ninety-six, yet still ending up three points behind Barcelona. *If I'd played all the games, would we have won?* Cristiano couldn't help but wonder. There was nothing for it but to keep training and trying.

ENTER MOURINHO

Portugal did not shine during the 2010 World Cup in South Africa, going out in the second round to Spain, with Cristiano only scoring one goal.

When he returned to Madrid for the 2010/11 season, there would be a new man in the manager's chair: José Mourinho, fresh from winning a Treble with Inter Milan.

Cristiano was disappointed not to have won anything the previous season, so redoubled his efforts in the gym and on the training pitch. It did not go unnoticed.

"He's a model professional," said Xabi Alonso.

"A machine," agreed goalkeeper Jerzy Dudek. "Always in more than an hour before training and then extra gym work."

Cristiano had been handed the number seven shirt for the new season, which he now also wore for Portugal. José was desperate to catch Barcelona that year, but a 5-0 hammering at their Camp Nou stadium in November did not bode well. Yet they managed to stay in touching distance in the league and found themselves playing Barca four times in a month at the end of the season, including in the Champions League. By that stage, Cristiano had already hit four league hat-tricks. Could he do it again?

He scored a penalty in a draw in the league, and in the end, Madrid couldn't reduce the points gap between the two teams. Four days later, they met in the Copa del Rey final, Spain's premier cup competition. After ninety minutes it remained goalless, with the game going to extra time. Who would win it? In the one-hundred-and-third minute Marcelo played a one-two with Ángel Di María, who put in a deep cross. It sailed over everyone. Well, nearly everyone. Waiting at the edge of the six-yard box was Cristiano, who jumped above his defender and connected with the ball. The net bulged. GOOOAALLLL!

He ran off in wild celebration as his teammates chased him. "Amazing!" cried Sergio Ramos.

"You've won it for us!" yelled Marcelo.

What a feeling – Cristiano's first Real Madrid trophy!

Unfortunately, Barcelona came out on top in the Champions League semi-final, and also clinched La Liga again. Yet Cristiano had had his best-ever goal-scoring year, with an incredible forty league goals and fifty-three in total. He felt even better when he learned he'd won the European Golden Shoe, the award given to the player who has scored the most goals in a European league. He'd won it in 2008 at Manchester United, but doing so with Madrid was a sign things were moving in the right direction.

They had come close to Barcelona again. Could they go one better next year?

HITTING A HUNDRED

The 2011/12 season would, once again, be closely contested with Madrid and Barcelona jostling for position at the top of the league. The last two seasons had been close, but Barca had pipped Madrid to the title both times. Cristiano was determined not to let it happen again.

By the first league meeting of the two clubs in December, Madrid were top of the league and Cristiano had already scored seventeen league goals, including four hat-tricks. Karim Benzema scored after twenty-two seconds, and things were looking good. But, drawing on all their experience,

Barca fought back to win 3-1. The Madrid fans were not happy and blamed Cristiano – they thought his price tag meant he had to win them every game. Some even booed him in their next two home matches.

Many players would be scared of making mistakes and struck by nerves when playing, but not Cristiano. *I will show them*, he thought. *I can do even more.* His strength and determination were about to be made clear to everyone.

Madrid did not lose a single league game before their next meeting with Barcelona in April, and Cristiano scored twenty-four more goals, including further hat-tricks against Sevilla, Levante and rivals Atlético Madrid. The stats were truly incredible. If they won this match – away at the Camp Nou – the title was as good as theirs.

Sami Khedira put the visitors ahead in the first half, but Barcelona equalized with a scrappy goal from Alexis Sánchez in the second. The teams were evenly matched, with Barca having more possession but restricted to shots from distance, while Madrid were dangerous on the counter-attack. In the seventy-third minute, Real launched yet another break from defence. Ángel laid the ball out to Mesut Özil on the right, just inside the Barcelona half. He looked up and saw Cristiano with his arm in the air, running between the centre backs. With a pinpoint pass, he laid the ball straight into Cristiano's path. Cristiano rounded the keeper and blasted it into the net. 2-1! A massive goal in the title race!

As his teammates ran over to him in delight, he said, "Calm down, guys! We're not there yet. Keep going."

When the final whistle blew, the Madrid players threw their arms up in the air. They had defeated what many people thought was the best club side ever. It was a great victory, their first away to Barcelona in a long time. The title was nearly in their grasp. Wins against Sevilla and Athletic Bilbao confirmed it – Madrid and Cristiano were champions of Spain!

The next two matches of the league no longer mattered, but Madrid won them anyway to finish on an historic one hundred points.

Cristiano had had a remarkable season and had only been spurred on by the boos of the Madrid fans. In fact, by the season's end, he was receiving standing ovations for his performances! He scored forty-six goals in La Liga and a whopping sixty in total. He was at the peak of his powers.

LA DECIMA

After the disappointment of crashing out of Euro 2012 on penalties against Spain, and dealing with criticism every time he didn't score for his country, Cristiano was ready for the new season in Madrid.

2012/13 saw him continue his brilliant goal-scoring form. He scored two goals in a draw at Barcelona and bagged hat-tricks against Deportivo La Coruña, Getafe and Sevilla. Despite this, they fell behind Barca early on in La Liga and never caught up.

The last sixteen of the Champions League allowed Cristiano to return to Old Trafford as a

Madrid player for the first time. He had scored the equalizer at the Bernabéu in a 1-1 draw, and slid in to grab the second in a 2-1 win at his old ground to send Madrid through to the quarters. He did not celebrate either goal as a mark of respect to his old club.

After the match, Cristiano went into the dressing room to see his old teammates. "What are you doing here? You knocked us out!" joked Rio Ferdinand.

"If you'd have celebrated the goal, I'd have throttled you," Sir Alex said to him after a hug. It was a happy reunion.

Madrid got no further than the semi-finals that season, losing to Borussia Dortmund. It was the third year on the run that they had lost at that stage. Cristiano and his teammates were determined to put that right.

While it was not a great season for Real Madrid – they had also lost in the final of the Copa del Rey to Atlético Madrid – Cristiano had performed brilliantly yet again, scoring fifty-five goals in as many matches.

For the 2013/14 season, José Mourinho

was replaced by the Italian Carlo Ancelotti as manager. Gareth Bale, the Welsh superstar from Tottenham Hotspur, was brought in for a world-record fee. With such big changes at the club, they simply had to win something. La Décima – Madrid's tenth European title – was their top priority.

Success didn't seem like it would come in La Liga again, with Atlético and Barcelona fighting it out for the title. Cristiano did reach his four-hundredth career goal in a match against Celta Vigo, though. Yet Madrid made good progress in the Copa del Rey, where they reached the final, and the Champions League, where they were to play Bayern Munich in the semis.

Before that, Cristiano was to see if his efforts in 2013 were enough for him to win a second Ballon d'Or and once again be recognized as the world's best player. It was what he had worked so hard for. Ahead of the ceremony, he was very nervous. He had scored sixty-nine goals in total that year, more than his arch-rival, Lionel Messi. The Argentinian had won the award for the last four years – would it finally be Cristiano's turn again?

Brazilian legend Pelé opened the envelope. "And the winner is … Cristiano Ronaldo!" The boy from Madeira experienced so many feelings flooding over him as he went up to accept the award.

"There are no words to describe this moment …" he said into the microphone. It was too much – the tears came. He struggled through his thank yous to teammates, family and friends while the audience applauded him. *I did it*, he thought.

The Copa del Rey final, yet again against Barcelona, was decided by a wonderful solo run from Gareth to win the game 2-1. Cristiano was dealing with an injury and cheered from the stands. "Amazing, Gareth! Well done!"

In Europe, Real hammered Bayern Munich, managed by former Barca boss Pep Guardiola, 5-0 over the two legs, with Cristiano scoring twice. They were in their first final in twelve years. And it would be against newly crowned La Liga champions Atlético, their Madrid city rivals.

It was a nervy match that both teams were scared to lose, but it was Atlético who went ahead in the first half. Cristiano was still struggling with an injury and had missed matches and barely trained to be on the pitch that day. As the game edged towards the final whistle, Real kept pressing. "Keep going!" Cristiano shouted. Deep into injury time, they had a corner. Luka Modrić curled it into the box – and Sergio got on the end of it to head it into the corner. Just in the nick of time it was 1-1!

Relief swept through Cristiano. "We're still in this – come on, boys!" he said as the game went to extra time. It seemed as though Atlético had spent all their energy in the regular ninety minutes. Real had a new lease of life and came forwards time and again. Eventually a clever run into the box and shot from Ángel forced a save from the Atlético keeper, which looped up only to be headed home by Gareth. 2-1! La Décima was on! Atlético spirits were broken, and Marcelo added a third a few minutes later.

There was still time for one more attack. Cristiano, desperate for another goal in a European final, tricked his way into the area, only to be brought down. Foul! Penalty! *This is my chance*, he thought. *Pick your spot and stick to it.* He ran up … and powered it into the right-hand corner! He was a champion of Europe again. He ripped off his shirt in celebration, and now the party could truly begin.

After years of trying, Cristiano and his teammates had finally delivered La Décima. It was worth the wait.

SIII!

At the 2014 World Cup in Brazil, Cristiano was still struggling from the injury suffered in the final two months of Madrid's season. Try as he might, he did not have the impact he wanted, and Portugal went out in the group stages.

He rested that summer and returned to a team on a roll. In December, Real won the Club World Cup, ending a wonderful 2014 for Cristiano with yet another trophy. He'd scored sixty-one goals, which was enough to secure another Ballon d'Or – his third, just one behind Messi's four.

Cristiano was over the moon – he'd continued

to work hard and had got his rewards. He ended his acceptance speech with a loud, "*Siiii!*" (Spanish for "yes"). This was what was shouted by Madrid players after great demonstrations of skill or special goals, and had been included as part of one of Cristiano's newer goal celebrations. It was certainly another special night for the Portuguese.

Madrid's roll, however, did not last as 2014 turned into 2015. A number of losses in the league allowed Barcelona to pinch the top spot, and a Champions League semi-final loss to Juventus ultimately meant that the season ended with disappointment. On a personal level, Cristiano's standards never dipped. He scored a staggering sixty-one goals in fifty-four matches, meaning he received the European Golden Shoe for the second year running – his fourth in total.

Yet his ambition was not necessarily matched by the amount of trophies Madrid had won. "Jorge, it's been six years – we should have won more! What can I do?" he asked his agent at dinner one evening.

"Your hard work and commitment have got you

this far. Keep it up and keep doing what you do best – scoring goals – and the trophies will come, trust me."

Jorge was right. By the end of the following season, Real found themselves in another Champions League final, once again against Atlético Madrid. Along the way, Cristiano had become Real Madrid's all-time record goal-scorer. He'd also reached five hundred career goals. Club legend Zinedine Zidane had taken over as manager halfway through the season, and his approach of giving freedom to Cristiano had paid off. The team had the chance for an eleventh European crown.

Another tight game ended 1-1 after extra time, with Sergio scoring Real's goal. Both sides exhausted huge amounts of energy over the course of the match. As Cristiano gathered with his teammates ahead of a penalty shoot-out, he said, "Guys, I'm dead. My legs aren't working." He wasn't the only one – half the team had a cramp.

"OK, who is up for the responsibility of a penalty?" Zinedine asked as he came over.

Despite his tiredness, Cristiano was the first

to volunteer. "Boss, let me go last. I will handle the pressure."

"I knew I could count on you, Cristiano. Who else? Lucas Vázquez, good. Marcelo? Sergio? Gareth? Great. You can all do this. Let's bring our trophy home."

Real scored their first four penalties. And then Juanfran of Atlético hit the post – he'd missed! It was Cristiano's chance to prove he could indeed handle the pressure. His teammates looked at each other. They remembered how tired he had said he was.

But on the big occasion, Cristiano knew he could deliver. He stared the keeper in the eyes, ran up and smashed his penalty high into the net. They'd done it again! They were champions of Europe! *How could it get any better than this?* Cristiano thought.

He was about to find out. Jorge was right – because it was only the beginning of Cristiano's winning run.

THE PINNACLE

"We will reach the final and we'll win it." This was what Portugal coach Fernando Santos had been saying for nearly two years during qualifying for Euro 2016 in France. Now the tournament had arrived, and he had not changed his tune. The words filled captain Cristiano and the rest of the squad with belief.

"I think we can do this," Cristiano said to his teammate Nani before their first game. "We have a good team, fantastic team spirit and a great coach."

Portugal only scraped through their group with three draws, but the main thing was that they were still alive and ready to fight. A second-round meeting with Croatia was again close, and was only decided by a Ricardo Quaresma goal in extra time.

It wasn't pretty football, but Cristiano knew they just had to stay in and keep going. As Fernando said, they would be in that final.

On to the next round, and Cristiano was heavily involved in the quarter-final against Poland, running and working tirelessly for his team. Another draw meant penalties yet again. The Portugal captain buried the first one, leading from the front as his country ran out 5-3 winners to move to the semis. "Come on, boys! We're doing this!" Cristiano said in the team talk after the match. "One game at a time. Stay focused."

The semi-final was against Wales, meaning Cristiano would face his teammate Gareth Bale. Wales had shocked everyone by making it this far, with Gareth playing some brilliant football. It was a difficult match for Cristiano to get into – Wales defended well and limited his chances. *Just give me one opportunity*, he thought, *and I can win this.* He had to believe.

In the fiftieth minute, João Mário took a corner

short to Raphaël Guerreiro, who whipped in an out-swinging cross. Cristiano saw the ball coming and leaped, hanging in the air. His connection was perfect. YESSSS! 1-0 to Portugal! They had one foot in the final, and it was about to get even better. Three minutes later, Cristiano's shot was diverted into the net by Nani – 2-0! Portugal had reached their first final since 2004.

Fernando's words had come true – they had reached the final – but they still had a job to do, and their whole country was behind them. It would be a huge challenge, because they were playing the tournament's hosts, France.

Expectation was at fever pitch for both the Portugal fans and the French. As Cristiano stood in the tunnel, waiting to lead his teammates on to the pitch, he thought about his long journey to this decisive moment. He thought about his family and friends, and how he hoped he'd do them proud. He'd come a long way from being the skinny boy playing on the sloping streets of Madeira. "Come on, boys! Remember the game plan!" shouted Nani behind him. *Here we go.*

The players were fired up after Fernando's team

talk. Unfortunately, France were also raring to go. Just a few minutes in, Cristiano received the ball. He tried to turn, but France's Dimitri Payet came steaming in, hitting Cristiano's knee and sending him to the ground. Foul! Only, this was no ordinary collision – the Portugal captain looked really hurt. Tears popped into his eyes as he feared his game might be over.

Try to run it off, he thought to himself. *Even if I'm not a hundred per cent, maybe I could still get a goal.* It was no use. A few minutes later, he collapsed to the floor again. It was time to admit defeat. He was carried off on a stretcher to sympathetic applause. No one wanted to see the world's best player going off injured.

"We'll do you proud. We'll put everything on the line for you," whispered Nani as Cristiano went off.

And they did just that. They stood firm against everything France could throw at them over the ninety minutes. Their team spirit was unshakeable. Into thirty minutes of extra time they went, with Cristiano hobbling among the players, offering words of encouragement before play started again. He remained glued to the touchline for most of extra time. Would they get the chance they needed?

In the one-hundred-and-ninth minute, striker Eder received the ball outside the penalty area. He took a couple of strides and shot ... GOAAAALLLLLL! Portugal were ahead! It was a brilliant strike from an unlikely hero. Now, could they hold on? On the sidelines, Cristiano was a bag of nerves. He was living every moment as France came again. But this was Portugal's time, and it was they who created the better chances in the final minutes. They drew upon all their experience and determination – they would not let this get away. They'd do it for their captain.

When the final whistle blew, Cristiano, the Portuguese team and their fans in the stadium and across the world let out a titanic roar of celebration. They had done it – they'd written history for their country.

GOLDEN YEARS

Cristiano's incredible 2016, in which he'd won the Champions League, the Euros and the Club World Cup again – with Cristiano scoring a hat-trick in the final – was rewarded with his fourth Ballon d'Or. By the end of the 2016/17 season, in which he'd often played as a central striker rather than a winger, he found himself with the opportunity to continue that winning streak. Madrid were in with a chance of both a league title and becoming the first team to win the Champions League two seasons running.

A goal for Cristiano in a 2-0 win over Málaga secured Madrid's first La Liga crown since 2012;

next up was the Champions League final against Juventus, and Cristiano was on an unstoppable roll, having hit an astonishing eight goals across the quarter- and semi-finals.

He continued his magnificent form in the final, scoring two more goals in a 4-1 victory over Juventus. Madrid were on top of the world. What's more, his goals in the final took his tally to six hundred for his career – incredible!

At the age of thirty-two, some people thought Cristiano might be getting too old to keep up such standards. But he had shown that with a formidable mindset and outstanding fitness, he could still achieve anything.

Despite again winning the Club World Cup at the end of 2017, this time thanks to a Cristiano free-kick winner, and Cristiano picking up his fifth Ballon d'Or, Madrid struggled in the league in 2017/18. It looked as though their achievements of the last two years had tired them out, but there was still some hope in the Champions League.

Madrid were drawn against Juventus in the quarter-final. Things had started well for Real in the first leg in Italy, with Cristiano scoring in just the third minute. What happened next would live long in everyone's memory. On a break, a Lucas Vázquez shot was saved by Juventus keeper Gianluigi Buffon. The ball flew out to Dani Carvajal on the right, who managed to float in a cross, but it was too far behind Cristiano for a headed attempt. So he decided to try something different. In a split second he turned his body so his back was facing the goal. He leaped, his feet reaching high in the air. As he floated above the ground, he volleyed the ball behind himself, past an astonished Buffon and into the bottom corner of the net. It was a truly spectacular goal. As Cristiano ran to the corner to celebrate, he heard the sound of applause. It came from everywhere. The Juventus fans were giving him a standing ovation! No one at the Italian club would forget that moment.

Madrid won the first leg 3-0, and survived a scare at home to sneak through to the semi-final, where they played Bayern Munich. Victory over the Germans meant Real had reached a third Champions League final on the run. Cristiano couldn't believe it.

"This is our tournament, our time. Let's make it

three!" he said before the players left the dressing room for the final. They were facing Liverpool, who were a team on the rise with fantastic players such as Sadio Mané and Mo Salah. Unfortunately for Liverpool, Salah had to go off injured in the first half. Cristiano really felt for him, remembering his own injury-hit final in Euro 2016.

But there couldn't be much time for sympathy – Madrid had a match to win. A gift of a goal from a Liverpool mistake put Real 1-0 up, but Liverpool showed they were still a threat when Sadio Mané equalized a few minutes later. Gareth Bale then popped up with a truly stunning overhead kick to make it 2-1. It was even better than Cristiano's against Juventus! Another Gareth goal with seven minutes to go sealed the tie, and Madrid remained kings of Europe.

When Cristiano was interviewed after the game, he said, "Now is the time to enjoy this … It has been very nice being at Real Madrid." Everyone was stunned. Was Cristiano leaving? Was it the end of an era?

KINGS OF EUROPE

The Champions League, previously known as the European Cup, is Europe's leading club competition. It has been played since the 1955/56 season and one team has won it more than any other: Real Madrid. They have been victorious a record fifteen times, including in the first five editions of the tournament, and most recently in 2024.

No one has ever appeared more times in the competition than Cristiano, or scored more goals. He has won the tournament on five occasions, putting him joint second, behind only a select few players, all legends of Real Madrid.

A NEW BEGINNING

On 10 July 2018, ten days after a second-round World Cup exit for Portugal, it was announced that Cristiano was joining Juventus. The Italian club would pay Real Madrid more than one-hundred million pounds – the biggest-ever fee for a player over the age of thirty. They hadn't forgotten the bicycle kick he'd scored against them a few months earlier, and hoped some of his magic would rub off on them and take them to European glory for the first time in more than twenty years.

It was tough to say goodbye to Madrid, but Cristiano knew he needed a new challenge. He thanked the players, the staff and the fans, and then it was off to Turin and the Italian league, Serie A. He was keen to see if he could also make it in Italy.

As always, he threw himself into his training, and quickly made an impact. In his fourth appearance, he scored his first two goals for Juventus in a 2-1 win over Sassuolo. By February 2019, he had scored in nine consecutive league away games – a joint record – and by April, he had helped his team get one game away from the Serie A title. They just needed a single point against Fiorentina, and when an opposition defender put Cristiano's cross into his own net, Juventus clinched the victory.

JUVENTUS

Club name: Juventus
Nickname: La Vecchia Signora (the Old Lady)
Founded: 1897
Current league: Serie A
Ground: Juventus Stadium (41,507 capacity)
Colours: Black and white stripes

"I'm very happy to have won in England, Spain and now the league title in Italy as well," said Cristiano afterwards. He had become the first player to do so – another record! "It meant a lot to me and it means a lot to us as a team."

His efforts that season – twenty-one goals in Serie A and twenty-eight overall – saw him named the league's Most Valuable Player.

But it didn't stop there. The next season, 2019/20, Cristiano contributed even more. A winning goal at Sampdoria saw him jump higher than the crossbar to score a header. Against all odds, at thirty-four years old he still had the speed and strength to score jaw-dropping goals. "Wow, wow, wow!" was the commentator's astonished reaction. In February, he played his thousandth senior game. It would be a special day, as he equalled the league record of scoring in consecutive matches when he netted for the eleventh game on the run. It might've been a new league, but it was the same old Cristiano!

In March 2020, Serie A was suspended due to the Covid-19 pandemic. This was a sad time for Cristiano, as he missed playing the game he loved and entertaining the fans. He knew he had to be ready when football returned, so kept training hard in the swimming pool and gym. When it did start again, Cristiano was raring to go. He kept banging the goals in, helping Juventus win the league again and finishing the season with a total of thirty-seven – the most ever scored in a single season by a Juventus player, breaking an eighty-year-old record.

Cristiano's third season in Italy, 2020/21, saw him win the award for Serie A's top scorer, with twenty-nine goals. He'd now scored more than one hundred goals for Juventus, doing it faster than any player before. That season, the club won the Coppa Italia, meaning Cristiano was the first player ever to win all the major trophies in England, Spain and Italy.

While records had tumbled in Italy, Cristiano felt it was again time to move on. For some time now, one particular club had been on his mind. One where he had enjoyed some of his greatest moments and where the fans still sung his name.

WELCOME BACK
TO MANCHESTER

The 2020 European Championships would be held a year late due to the effects of the Covid pandemic. Cristiano was off to a flyer, scoring five goals in group games against Hungary, Germany and France. Portugal went out in the round of sixteen, but their captain's efforts still saw him end with the Golden Boot for the tournament's top scorer. Not bad for a thirty-six-year-old!

After a short break, it was back to Turin and Juventus, but it wouldn't be for long. On 27 August 2021, Manchester United announced they had re-signed one of their greatest ever players. Cristiano would be heading back to Old Trafford! His unexpected signing sent United fans wild with joy. What's more, striker Edinson Cavani agreed to give up his number seven shirt and take number twenty-one – Cristiano would get his old number back!

"I can't even start to explain my feelings right now, as I see my return to Old Trafford announced worldwide. It's like a dream come true … to have always felt such love and respect from the supporters in the stands. This is absolutely one hundred per cent the stuff that dreams are made of!" he wrote on social media. He was back!

United supporters couldn't believe it. After a few years of disappointment since Sir Alex Ferguson had retired, Cristiano's arrival had lifted the spirits. The team was managed by Cristiano's old teammate Ole Gunnar Solksjær now, and after a promising season with great players such as Bruno Fernandes and Marcus Rashford, United were looking to challenge for trophies again. Would Cristiano be the missing piece of the puzzle?

It started off well. His second debut came on 11 September, and Old Trafford was at fever pitch with excitement as the fans watched their old – and now new – number seven walk out on to the pitch. Newcastle United were the opponents and Cristiano was feeling ruthless. On the stroke of half-time he pounced on a spilled shot from the Newcastle keeper to poke the ball home. The fans were loving it – 1-0! "Yeeessss!" cried Cristiano as he turned and jumped in the air to celebrate.

Another goal in the second half showed his pace and power as he raced on to a Luke Shaw through ball to drill it past the goalie. "Incredible!" shouted Bruno to his Portuguese teammate.

"It could only be him!" said the commentators. A 4-1 win had truly announced Cristiano's second coming.

A few weeks later the dream return continued with a last-minute winner to beat Villarreal 2-1 in the Champions League. Cristiano did the same again at home against Atalanta in the next European game, coming back from 2-0 down to win 3-2; and yet another last-minute Cristiano goal saw United grab the equalizer in the fixture away from home. It was getting ridiculous!

Things were going less well in the league, though, with bad losses against rivals Liverpool and Manchester City, as well as Watford. This saw Cristiano's friend Ole sacked as manager, to be replaced by German Ralf Rangnick for the rest of the season. Cristiano continued to try his best, scoring two in a win against Arsenal to take him to eight-hundred career goals, and hat-tricks against Tottenham and Norwich at home. But unfortunately, United finished the season in sixth place, missing out on Champions League qualification and without a trophy.

Cristiano ended the season as United's top scorer, with eighteen in the league – only putting him behind Mo Salah and Son Heung-min – and twenty-four overall. Although he had done well, it was ultimately a disappointing season. He hoped things would turn around when the new manager, Erik ten Hag, arrived that summer from Ajax.

Cristiano did not play as much as he would have liked to at the start of the 2022/23 season, and he began to wonder if this meant his time back at Old Trafford might be coming to an end. He did score twice in the Europa League and in a win over Everton, but sadly these proved to be his last performances in a United shirt. The new manager had detailed plans for his squad and the club, and Cristiano realized he wasn't a big part of them. Everyone agreed it was best if Cristiano went to a club where he would play more regularly. In November, just after the start of the 2022 World Cup, his contract was ended.

It was a disappointing finish to his United career, but Cristiano still looks back on his time at the club with pride: he won his first league title, his first Champions League and his first Ballon d'Or there, so it will always hold a special place in his heart.

ONE FINAL CHALLENGE

After playing in his fifth World Cup in Qatar, where he struck the back of the net to become the first ever player to score in five editions of the tournament, Cristiano was looking for his next club. Portugal had gone out at the quarter-final stage, with Cristiano losing his place in the starting line-up. *I need a new challenge, where I can start fresh and show people I am still a great player*, he thought. It had been a non-stop few years. Clubs from many countries were interested in him, but it was Saudi Arabia's Al Nassr that won his heart.

AL NASSR

Club name: Al Nassr
Nickname: Al-Alami (the Global One)
Founded: 1955
Current league: Pro League
Ground: Al-Awwal Park (25,000 capacity)
Colours: Yellow and blue

He knew this was a region where he could help grow the popularity of the game. "In Europe, my work is done. I won everything, I played at the most important clubs in Europe and for me now, it's a new challenge ... Many clubs tried to sign me, but I gave my word to this club to develop not only the football, but other parts of this amazing country," he said after he signed. He wanted to be part of something new, something exciting, and Al Nassr was the perfect club to do this at.

His new team finished as league runners-up in his first season, but he showed everyone he still knew how to find the back of the net with fourteen goals in just sixteen games. That summer of 2023 showed just what Cristiano had meant about developing Saudi Arabia's football. Many top players from around Europe decided to join the Saudi Pro League once they saw Cristiano lead the way. His old teammate Karim Benzema, plus Neymar, Sadio Mané, N'Golo Kanté, Riyad Mahrez and Roberto Firmino all joined Saudi teams from big clubs. The league was going places.

In his second season, Cristiano helped Al Nassr win their first ever Arab Club Champions Cup by scoring both goals in the final. He still had that big-game magic! By the end of the 2023/24 season, he had scored thirty-five goals for his club, his best year since 2016. This meant he also became the first footballer to finish as top scorer in four different leagues.

And who knows how many more Cristiano may score? What more can we expect from him? The only records he has left to break are now his own. By appearing for Portugal in Euro 2024, he became the first player to feature in six European Championships, having previously been the first player to appear in five! He continues to silence the critics with his abilities and still sets the pace for younger players. While the desire to keep scoring burns brightly, he will carry on. Of course, a day will come when he does hang up his boots – but that day is not today.

Cristiano Ronaldo's Timeline

5 February 1985   Ronaldo dos Santos Aveiro is born in Funchal, Madeira.

1992   He joins Andorinha football club as an eight-year-old.

1995   Aged ten, his godfather Fernão Barros Sousa, Nacional's youth-team coach, watches Cristiano play. The boy soon signs for Nacional.

April 1997   He takes his first flight, alone, to mainland Portugal for a three-day trial with Sporting.

August 1997	His mother, Dolores, signs a three-year training contract for twelve-year-old Cristiano to move to Sporting. The fee paid to Nacional is 1,500 euros.
June 2000	He has heart surgery to correct a racing heart condition.
2001/2002	Aged sixteen, he becomes the first player in Sporting history to play for the Under-16s, Under 17s, Under-18s, reserves and first team in the same season.
2002	He signs his first professional contract.
14 August 2002	He makes his Sporting first-team debut in a Champions League qualifying match against Inter Milan.
September 2002	Jorge Mendes becomes his new agent.
29 September 2002	He makes his league debut against Sporting Braga.

7 October 2002	Cristiano scores his first senior goals in a 3-0 win against Moreirense.
6 August 2003	He plays for Sporting in a pre-season friendly versus Manchester United, where an agreement is made for a transfer.
12 August 2003	He is signed for Manchester United for a fee of 12.24 million pounds.
16 August 2003	He makes his Manchester United debut in a Premier League game against Bolton Wanderers, wins his side a penalty and is given the Man of the Match award.
20 August 2003	He makes his first senior appearance for Portugal, coming on as a substitute in a match against Kazakhstan.
1 November 2003	He scores his first United goal from a free kick against Portsmouth.

22 May 2004	He wins his first trophy as a professional player after scoring the opener in a 3-0 win over Millwall in the FA Cup final.
12 June 2004	He scores his first international goal in Euro 2004, his first major tournament, in a loss to Greece.
4 July 2004	He starts for Portugal as they reach the Euro final against Greece, who again beat Portugal.
26 February 2006	He scores the third goal in a 4-0 win over Wigan Athletic to lift the League Cup.
Summer 2006	He plays in his first World Cup, where Portugal reach the semi-final. He is criticized by the English fans and media for his part in club mate Wayne Rooney's red card.
10 April 2007	He scores his first Champions League goal in a 7-1 win over Roma in the quarter-final.

6 May 2007	He wins his first league title after Chelsea draw with Arsenal.
August/September 2007	He has one-to-one training sessions with first-team coach René Meulensteen, aimed at improving his finishing skills.
12 January 2008	He scores his first hat-trick in a 6-0 win against Newcastle United in the Premier League.
1 April 2008	He scores an incredible header in the Champions League quarter-final first leg against Roma. The goal helps secure an aggregate 3-0 win.
11 May 2008	He scores in a 2-0 win over Wigan Athletic to help United retain the Premier League. His thirty-one league goals earn him the Premier League Golden Boot.

21 May 2008	He scores his side's goal in a 1-1 draw with Chelsea in the Champions League final. Cristiano misses his penalty but United triumph, winning him his first European title. His forty-two goals secure him the European Golden Shoe.
July 2008	Cristiano is made Portugal's captain. His team go out in the quarter-final of Euro 2008.
15 November 2008	He scores his hundredth United goal with a free kick against Stoke City.
2 December 2008	He wins the Ballon d'Or, finally making his dream to be the world's best footballer a reality.
21 December 2008	He helps United win their first Club World Cup.
1 March 2009:	He scores his penalty in a shoot-out win over Tottenham Hotspur to lift the League Cup.

15 April 2009	He scores an incredible forty-yard strike in a 1-0 victory over Porto to send United to the Champions League semi-final. The goal wins the FIFA Puskás Award.
11 June 2009	He is transferred to Real Madrid for a world-record fee of eighty-million pounds.
29 August 2009	He makes his Real Madrid debut and scores his first goal with a penalty in a 3-2 win against Deportivo La Coruña.
5 May 2010	He scores his first Madrid hat-trick, against Real Mallorca.
17 June 2010	His first child, Cristiano Ronaldo Junior, is born in the United States.
29 June 2010	Portugal lose to Spain in the last sixteen of the World Cup.
23 October 2010	He scores four goals in a 6-1 win over Racing Santander.

20 April 2011	He scores the only goal of the Copa del Rey final to beat Barcelona and win his first trophy for Madrid.
May 2011	He wins the European Golden Shoe for the second time with forty league goals, and fifty-four overall that season.
21 April 2012	He scores the winning goal at Barcelona to take Madrid to the brink of winning La Liga.
2 May 2012	Madrid are crowned Spanish champions after a 3-0 win at Athletic Bilbao – Cristiano's first La Liga win. Two more wins take Madrid to a record hundred-point tally.
27 June 2012	Portugal draw with Spain 0-0 in the semi-final, but lose on penalties. Cristiano is criticized for not taking one after he chooses to go last.

3 October 2012	He scores his first Champions League hat-trick in a 4-1 win at Ajax.
5 March 2013	He returns to Old Trafford for the first time since leaving United, scoring the winning goal in a 2-1 Champions League last-sixteen match. He does not celebrate.
19 November 2013	He scores a stunning hat-trick against Sweden in qualifying to send Portugal to the 2014 World Cup.
13 January 2014	He wins his second Ballon d'Or for a brilliant 2013, in which he scored sixty-nine goals.
May 2014	He wins his third European Golden Shoe for scoring thirty-one league goals in the season.
24 May 2014	He helps Madrid achieve La Décima by scoring a penalty in a 4-1 win over city rivals Atlético after extra time.

12 January 2015	He receives his third Ballon d'Or for a season in which he scored sixty-one goals.
5 April 2015	He scores five goals in a game for the first time in a 9-1 win over Granada.
May 2015	He wins his fourth European Golden Shoe for scoring an incredible forty-eight goals in La Liga that season.
30 September 2015	He scores his five-hundredth career goal in a 2-0 win at Malmö in the Champions League.
17 October 2015	He becomes Madrid's all-time top scorer with a goal against Levante to take his total to three-hundred-and-twenty-four goals.
28 May 2016	He scores the winning penalty in a shoot-out victory over Atlético Madrid in the Champions League final – his third European crown.

10 July 2016	He is forced off with injury in the Euro 2016 final. He patrols the touchline as Portugal win in extra time. Lifting the trophy is the pinnacle of his career.
12 December 2016	He wins his fourth Ballon d'Or for his achievements with Madrid and Portugal that year.
18 December 2016	He scores a hat-trick in the final of the Club World Cup.
21 May 2017	He scores as Madrid beat Málaga 2-0 to secure La Liga.
3 June 2017	After scoring hat-tricks in the quarters and semis, Cristiano nets twice in a 4-1 victory over Juventus in the Champions League final. The second is his six-hundredth career goal.
8 June 2017	He becomes a father to twins, Eva and Mateo.

12 November 2017	Cristiano and his partner, Georgina Rodriguez, announce the birth of their daughter Alana.
7 December 2017	He wins his fifth Ballon d'Or, tying with Lionel Messi.
16 December 2017	He scores a free-kick winner to beat Grêmio and help Madrid retain the Club World Cup.
18 March 2018	He scores his fiftieth career hat-trick with four goals in a 6-3 win at Girona.
3 April 2018	He scores a stunning bicycle kick at Juventus in the Champions League quarter-final.
26 May 2018	He wins his fifth Champions League as Madrid beat Liverpool to win the tournament for the third season running.
30 June 2018	Portugal are knocked out by Uruguay in the last sixteen at the World Cup in Russia.

10 July 2018	Cristiano transfers to Juventus for one-hundred million euros, the highest-ever fee for a player over thirty years old.
16 September 2018	He scores his first goals for Juventus in a 2-1 win over Sassuolo.
20 April 2019	His involvement in the winning goal against Fiorentina helps Juventus win Serie A. He is the first player to win league titles in England, Spain and Italy.
9 June 2019	He captains Portugal to victory in the first ever Nations League final.
6 January 2020	He scores his first Serie A hat-trick in a 4-0 win against Cagliari.
22 February 2020	In his thousandth senior game, he scores for a record-equalling eleventh Italian league game in a row.

26 July 2020	He scores in a 2-0 win over Sampdoria that sees Juventus win Serie A again.
7 August 2020	He finishes the season with thirty-seven goals, breaking a Juventus record for most goals in a season.
12 May 2021	He scores his hundredth Juventus goal in a 3-1 win at Sassuolo.
19 May 2021	Juventus win the Coppa Italia, making Cristiano the first player to win all major domestic tournaments in England, Spain and Italy. He also finishes the season as Serie A's top scorer.
June 2021	He scores five goals in the group stage of Euro 2020, which earns him the Golden Boot.
27 August 2021	Cristiano returns to Manchester United for a 12.85-million-pound fee.

11 September 2021	He makes his second United debut, scoring two goals in a 4-1 win over Newcastle.
2 December 2021	He scores two goals in a league victory over Arsenal, with the first taking him to eight-hundred career goals.
18 April 2022	His fifth child, Bella, is born.
22 November 2022	It is agreed his contract at Manchester United will be ended.
24 November 2022	He scores a penalty against Ghana to become the first man to score in five different World Cups.
30 December 2022	Cristiano agrees to join Saudi Arabian club Al Nassr.
4 February 2023	He scores his first goal for Al Nassr with an injury-time penalty against Al Fateh.
9 February 2023	He scores all four goals in a 4-0 win over Al-Wehda.

12 August 2023	He scores both goals as Al Nassr defeat Al Hilal 2-1 to win the Arab Club Champions Cup for the first time.
15 March 2024	He scores his fiftieth Al Nassr goal with a penalty in a 1-0 win over Al-Ahli.
18 June 2024	He becomes the first ever player to appear at six European Championships.

TEAM TROPHIES

DOMESTIC

Manchester United Premier League: 2006/07, 2007/08, 2008/09
FA Cup: 2003/04
League Cup: 2005/06, 2008/09
UEFA Champions League: 2007/08
FIFA Club World Cup: 2008

Real Madrid La Liga: 2011/12, 2016/17
Copa del Rey: 2010/11, 2013/14
UEFA Champions League: 2013/14, 2015/16, 2016/17, 2017/18
UEFA Super Cup: 2014, 2016, 2017
FIFA Club World Cup: 2014, 2016, 2017

Juventus	Serie A: 2018/19, 2019/20
	Coppa Italia: 2020/21
Al Nassr	Arab Club Champions Cup: 2023

INTERNATIONAL

| **Portugal** | UEFA European Championship: 2016 |
| | UEFA National League: 2018/19 |

INDIVIDUAL HONOURS

Premier League Player of the Season: 2006/07,
                                         2007/08

Professional Footballers' Association
Players' Player of the Year: 2006/07,
                                         2007/08

Premier League Golden Boot: 2007/08

European Golden Shoe: 2007/08,
                                         2010/11,
                                         2013/14,
                                         2014/15

UEFA Champions League top scorer:	2007/08, 2012/13, 2013/14, 2014/15, 2015/16, 2016/17, 2017/18
UEFA Club Footballer of the Year/ UEFA Men's Player of the Year:	2007/08, 2013/14, 2015/16, 2016/17
Ballon d'Or:	2008, 2013, 2014, 2016, 2017
FIFA World Player of the Year/ The Best FIFA Men's Player:	2008, 2016, 2017
FIFA Puskás Award:	2009

Pichichi Trophy (La Liga top scorer):	2010/11, 2013/14, 2014/15
La Liga Best Player	2013/14
FIFA Club World Cup Golden Ball:	2016
Serie A Footballer of the Year:	2019, 2020
Golden Foot:	2020
Capocannoniere (Serie A top scorer):	2020/21
UEFA European Championship Golden Boot:	2020 (played in 2021)

Cristiano's Clubs

SPORTING CP

Nickname: Leões (Lions)

Founded: 1906

Current league: Primeira Liga

Ground: Estádio José Alvalade (50,095 capacity)

Colours: Green and white

MANCHESTER UNITED

Nickname: The Red Devils, United

Founded: 1878

Current league: Premier League

Ground: Old Trafford (74,310 capacity)

Colours: Red, white and black

REAL MADRID

Nickname: Nickname: Los Blancos (the Whites), Los Merengues (the Meringues)

Founded: 1902

Current league: La Liga

Ground: Estadio Santiago Bernabéu (85,000 capacity)

Colours: White

JUVENTUS

Nickname: La Vecchia Signora (the Old Lady)

Founded: 1897

Current league: Serie A

Ground: Juventus Stadium (41,507 capacity)

Colours: Black and white stripes

AL NASSR

Nickname: Al-Alami (the Global One)

Founded: 1955

Current league: Pro League

Ground: Al-Awwal Park (25,000 capacity)

Colours: Yellow and blue

WHAT THEY SAY ABOUT CRISTIANO

"The way he faced competition, his courage, he wasn't deterred by anyone, whether they were older or younger than him. He just wanted to win; he hated to lose." — **António Mendonça**, Cristiano's coach at Nacional in 1995/96

"Cristiano Ronaldo was the greatest Man United athlete I ever coached." — Former United power development coach **Mike Clegg**

"He [Cristiano] does things I have never seen from any other player." — **Sir Bobby Charlton**

"There have been a few players described as the new George Best over the years, but this is the first time it's been a compliment to me." — **George Best**

"[Cristiano Ronaldo] is the most ambitious footballer I have ever met." — **Valter di Salvo**, former Real Madrid fitness coach

"He has an extraordinary physical and mental capacity … What I would most [emphasize] is his passion for sports, for his profession and his desire for self-improvement." — **Rafael Nadal**

"There are some things Ronaldo can do with a football that makes me touch my head and wonder how on earth he did it." — **Luís Figo**

"He's the best." — **Alfredo Di Stéfano**

"When you play with Ronaldo on your team, you are already 1-0 up." — **Zinedine Zidane**

"I think he is the best example in the world in terms of work ethic and winning mentality. Playing with this type of player, you improve every day." — **Raphaël Varane**

"[Cristiano] is always there scoring goals in all the games ... He has been doing that for many years and whether he is at his peak or a bit below it makes no difference." — **Lionel Messi**

WHAT CRISTIANO SAYS

"Talent without working hard is nothing."

"If you don't believe you are the best then you will never achieve all that you are capable of."

"Being captain of the Portuguese national team is being myself. It's not shying away from a fight, always giving your best, and fighting from the first to the last minute."

"I like being the most expensive player in the world. People say: 'You've got more pressure, more responsibility,' but that's already a part of it. Even if I weren't the most expensive player, I'd have the same responsibility."

"I love football. It's my life. Without this, without football, I don't know what to do. It's my life and I want to win everything I can."

"I hope to be on the first page of the history of football, on the same page as Maradona and Pelé. I want to get there ... I know it's hard, but in my mind it's possible."

FAMILY

Above all, Cristiano has always been a family man. Coming from a poor family meant his upbringing on Madeira was tough, but his success on the football pitch allowed him to give his family lives they otherwise wouldn't have had. A lot of his motivation to succeed comes from wanting to help them.

One of Cristiano's dreams was to have a big family and, in 2010, he became a father when his son Cristiano Ronaldo Junior was born. Seven years later he felt blessed to have two more children – Eva and Mateo.

In 2016, he met his long-term partner, Georgina Rodríguez. They quickly fell in love and welcomed their daughter Alana to the growing family. And things were to get even better – and bigger – when Cristiano's fifth child, Bella, was born in April 2022.

No matter where Cristiano is playing football, his family are rarely far from his thoughts, and he is never happier than when he is spending time with them.

CHARITY

Cristiano has given money to many charities and causes over the years, a lot of them aimed at helping children in poverty. He is an ambassador for UNICEF and World Vision, which help to improve children's lives.

After the 2004 tsunami devastated Indonesia, Cristiano travelled to the country to raise funds to help fix some of the damage. In 2009, after his mother, Dolores, had survived cancer, he donated one hundred thousand pounds to the Madeiran hospital that saved her life so they could build a cancer centre on the island. Cristiano also donated five million pounds to help people suffering after the Nepal earthquake in 2015. In 2020, he was moved to give another nine hundred thousand pounds to help buy medical supplies and support healthcare workers in Portugal during the Covid-19 pandemic.

During his career, Cristiano has given away many of his football bonuses to charity, auctioned one of his Ballon d'Or trophies and a Golden Boot to pay for building schools and hospitals in Africa and the Middle East, visited people in need in orphanages and hospitals, and used his voice to raise awareness about child labour and giving blood. He has even paid for people's cancer treatments and donated bone marrow.

Cristiano also cares for the natural world, and became an ambassador for the Mangrove Care Forum in Indonesia, which aims to protect mangroves, an important tree for slowing climate change.

Also available in the Football Legends series:

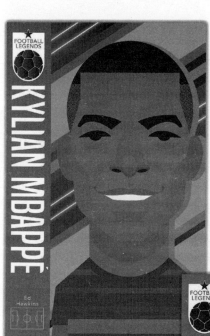

FOOTBALL
LEGENDS

KYLIAN MBAPPÉ

Ed
Hawkins

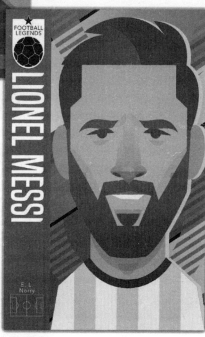

FOOTBALL
LEGENDS

LIONEL MESSI

E. L.
Norry

BUKAYO SAKA

Ben Lerwill

JUDE BELLINGHAM

Paul Stewart